MIKAL KEEFER

FOREWORD BY **RICK LAWRENCE**

# GROWING
## SPIRITUAL GRIT

### FOR TEENAGERS

40 DEVOTIONS

# Group | lifetree

**Growing Spiritual Grit for Teenagers**

40 Devotions

Copyright © 2018 Group Publishing, Inc./0000 0001 0362 4853

Lifetree™ is an imprint of Group Publishing, Inc.

Visit our website: group.com

### Credits

Author: Mikal Keefer

Chief Creative Officer: Joani Schultz

Senior Editor: Candace McMahan

Assistant Editor: Cherie Shifflett

Art Director and Designer: Jeff Storm

Production Artist: Andy Towler

Unless otherwise indicated, all Scripture quotations are taken from the Holy Bible, New Living Translation, copyright © 1996, 2004, 2007, 2013, 2015 by Tyndale House Foundation. Used by permission of Tyndale House Publishers, Inc., Carol Stream, Illinois 60188. All rights reserved.

ISBN: 978-1-4707-5337-5 (softcover), 978-1-4707-5546-1 (ePub)

Printed in the USA.

10 9 8 7 6 5 4 3 2 1          27 26 25 24 23 22 21 20 19 18

# CONTENTS

# FOREWORD

Finals. Dating weirdness. Family meltdowns.

Life is full of tough stuff.

We need strength and perseverance to navigate the rough terrain of life. And along the way, we discover that our own strength and perseverance are often not enough.

We need something bigger and tougher. We need grit.

Grit is the engine that drives perseverance. It's the core strength that helps us face and overcome challenges and obstacles. And it's the essential characteristic that sustains our lifelong journey with Jesus.

Without grit, our faith wavers, distractions derail us, and our focus blurs.

And here's the kicker: Every person who has had a great impact on the world, everyone who's lived out the mission and work of Jesus in world-changing ways, needed grit to do it. In fact, they needed a supercharged version of grit that's stronger than the garden-variety stuff we all develop along the way.

That "regular" grit helps us hang tough when we're tempted to quit. It helps us solve difficult problems that seem too big to overcome. But personal grit is limited by our capabilities; *spiritual* grit is fed by the limitless resources of Jesus and is anchored in a growing dependence on him.

When we're captured by a passion for Jesus, we not only take on the tough stuff, but we also discover joy in the journey because Jesus is our intimate companion.

And as daunting as all of this might sound, you're about to be shocked by how fun growing spiritual grit can be.

**Rick Lawrence**
Author of *Spiritual Grit*

# INTRODUCTION

These devotions will make you uncomfortable.

That's because you'll be doing the very things Jesus asked his first followers to do. Hard things, but things that ultimately gave those disciples the fortitude to own their faith, stand strong, and follow Jesus no matter what.

These devotions will help you grow grit. *Spiritual* grit.

And you develop spiritual grit much as you develop grit anywhere else in your life: by doing stuff.

Hard stuff.

Hard stuff that turns out to be good for you. That helps you rely on Jesus and see him working in and through you.

**Hard** = **Good**, at least in the kingdom of God.

You'll move outside your comfort zone, out to where you can see Jesus more clearly. You'll have conversations you haven't had before, look at people through new lenses, lean into challenging things.

You'll risk relying on Jesus.

You get two options in each devotion: to do something gritty and to do something even grittier. Feel free to do one or both. Ask Jesus what he recommends.

You'll then reflect on what you've experienced and talk it over with Jesus. That's a grit-builder, too.

Don't worry; there's nothing here that will leave scars. But you *will* stretch—in a good way. In a spiritually gritty way.

So take a deep breath...and let's get started.

Let's grow a little grit.

# KEEP THE FAITH—
# AND TRUST JESUS

It's several years into Jesus' ministry, and the disciples can see the wheels are falling off.

The crowds have thinned. Religious leaders Jesus has offended along the way are circling around like wolves closing in for the kill.

And Jesus seems unable—or maybe unwilling—to do anything about it. Even after he's publicly criticized. Even after a crowd in the Temple courtyard tries to stone him to death.

Even as the disciples point out the obvious: Jerusalem is no place for Jesus—or them. They'll be walking into a lions' den the moment they cross back into Judea.

But Jesus isn't persuaded. He's going to Judea and on into Jerusalem with or without them.

So it's up to the disciples to decide: Do they trust Jesus enough to follow him when everything they see tells them to cut their losses and walk away?

There's no question that they believe in Jesus, that they have faith. The miracles they've seen, the teaching they've heard, the healings that made Jesus famous—all of that convinced them long ago that he is who he says he is.

But when their lives are on the line, do they *trust* him?

Thomas' response to the dilemma is classic. He takes a long, deep breath and then sighs, "Let's go, too—and die with Jesus" (John 11:16).

Then this band of brothers, this dozen disciples, silently falls into step behind Jesus.*

Jesus' first disciples don't just have faith in Jesus—they trust him. And faith and trust are less alike than they appear at first glance.

Having faith isn't actually all that hard.

You can easily have faith that an ancient elevator creaking open in front of you is safe. It's carried passengers for decades, it was installed back when things were built to last, and some inspector has signed off that the floor's solid and the cables aren't frayed.

But when you step into the elevator and punch a button for the 30th floor, that's when faith turns into trust.

Faith prompts a nod of agreement. Trust prompts action.

If that's true, if trust translates into something that can be seen, heard, touched—what can you point to in your life that indicates you trust Jesus?

Good news: You'll soon be able to point to one or both of the experiences you'll find below.

## GRIT GROWER 1: TRUST WALK

You may be more trusting than you think.

Not sure about that?

Do this: Walk around your house or apartment and briefly touch everything you trust, often without even being aware you trust it.

That medicine bottle: You trust that the pharmacist didn't accidentally substitute cyanide.

The electric outlet? You trust it will work when you plug in your laptop.

*Read the entire account in John 11:1-16.*

And that website where you learn about the world? You trust that what you see is the truth, nothing but the truth and…well, maybe you don't trust *everything* in your house.

And that's okay: It's wise to trust carefully.

See how many objects—or people—you touch in a five-minute trust walk.

## AND EVEN GRITTIER

Take a virtual hike through the contact list on your phone. How much do you trust each of the people whose names scroll past?

Who's trustworthy? mostly trustworthy? less trustworthy?

And how do you decide where each name falls on your trust scale?

Now consider this: If Jesus did this same exercise and your name scrolled past, how do you think he'd rank your name on his list of trustworthiness? Why?

## TALK WITH JESUS

Jot your thoughts about…

- **What did you discover about yourself and trust?**

- **What did you discover about Jesus?**

- **What—if anything—would Jesus have to say or do to increase your trust in him?**

- Where was the spiritual grit in these experiences? You've now grown as a result of what you've done. What's different about you now, and why?

## GRIT GROWER 2: TRUSTING FOR THE RIGHT WORDS

There's a reason we love coming up with plans and then asking Jesus to put his stamp of approval on them: It means we're in control.

Which isn't all that trusting. Or grit-growing. Or God-honoring.

So do this: Pick up your phone.

Ask Jesus who he'd have you call—and why.

It could be someone who needs to feel remembered. Or maybe it's someone whose friendship with you is strained. It could be someone you've never met.

Listen for Jesus' voice. Be open to a face floating into focus.

Trust that what comes to mind was prompted by Jesus...and make the call.

## AND EVEN GRITTIER

It's time for a field trip.

If possible, take another Jesus-follower with you so you can talk about the experience afterward. But if that doesn't work, it's no problem.

You won't be alone.

Go to the nearest hospital emergency room, and when you get to the door, pray this: "Jesus, for the next hour, I'm at your disposal. You lead, and I'll follow."

Then walk in, find a seat in the waiting area, and trust that Jesus will tell you what's next.

Maybe he'll ask you to pray for that woman weeping in the corner. Or to strike up a conversation with the angry man pacing the room.

Trust Jesus for direction. For the right words. For whatever's coming next.

## TALK WITH JESUS

Jot your thoughts about...

- **What did you discover about yourself through these experiences?**

- **What did you discover about trusting Jesus?**

- **In what ways does putting yourself out there without a plan build your trust in Jesus?**

- **Where was the spiritual grit in these experiences? How are you different as a result of these experiences, and why?**

## GRIT GROWER 3: TELL A SECRET

And not just any secret.

Tell a *secret* secret—one that would complicate your life if it were whispered around. That would scuttle your ship if it were posted to social media.

The sort of secret you've walled off inside yourself. That you haven't shared with many people...maybe with anyone, ever.

A secret that's a weight, a chain around your heart.

Find a place where you can speak out loud and not be heard. Then share that secret with Jesus. Hear yourself say it aloud.

Picture his face as he listens to you. What's that you see in his eyes?

## AND EVEN GRITTIER

Tell that same secret to a person—a person you trust.

Who? That's up to you, but beware: You're putting your comfort, perhaps even your future, in that person's hands.

So choose wisely.

What's the secret? And who's the person?

## TALK WITH JESUS

Jot your thoughts about…

- **What did you discover about yourself through these experiences?**

- **What did you discover about trusting others?**

- **How trusting would you say your relationship with Jesus is? Why do you answer as you do?**

- **Where was the spiritual grit in these experiences? What strength (even a little) have you gained?**

# LOVE YOUR ENEMIES— ALL OF THEM

Now and then Jesus says something that makes his disciples miserable.

For instance, imagine how they feel when they hear this:

"You have heard the law that says, 'Love your neighbor and hate your enemy.'

"But I say, love your enemies! Pray for those who persecute you! In that way, you will be acting as true children of your Father in heaven.

"For he gives his sunlight to both the evil and the good, and he sends rain on the just and the unjust alike.

"If you love only those who love you, what reward is there for that? Even corrupt tax collectors do that much. If you are kind only to your friends, how are you different from anyone else? Even pagans do that.

"But you are to be perfect, even as your Father in heaven is perfect" (Matthew 5:43-48).

Jesus' disciples trade a few uncomfortable glances hearing those words. They've traveled together, and you know how guys talk—they've shared stories about who's on their naughty and nice lists.

And they *have* been praying about their enemies—but not the way Jesus commands. They've been praying more about enemies getting hit with lightning than blessings.*

To want the best for people who've hurt you? That's gritty.

To actively seek *good* for those enemies? Back up the wheelbarrow—that's a big ol' *pile* of grit.

Clearly, as far as enemies are concerned, the first disciples are in need of an attitude adjustment...and they're not alone.

Jesus calls his followers—including you—to love others as God loves you. To pass along what you've received. To actively seek what's best for others even if they don't acknowledge or appreciate it.

Hard? Try impossible, at least on your own.

It takes grace. And if you've tried grace-filled living, you know you can't pull it off on your own.

But here's the good news: You're *not* on your own. You're following Jesus, and he's in this with you.

Grace is powered by Jesus himself; it's his fingerprints on the world. When you experience grace—on either the giving or receiving end—you know Jesus can't be far away.

When's the last time you spotted Jesus' fingerprints on your life?

## GRIT GROWER 4: MAKE AN ENEMIES LIST

Maybe no one's paying an assassin to poison your pasta, but there are people who don't wish you well. Or who ignore you.

Those are your enemies.

That girl who trashes you on social media. The teacher who loves making fun of you in front of others.

That person who damaged you years ago, whose wounds still sting. What happened may be in the past, but so far, you're not past it.

*Read the entire account in Matthew 5:31-48.*

Your enemy is anyone who's hurt you, whether deliberately or by willful indifference. Anyone on that list—*everyone* on it—is who Jesus expects you to love.

Not just tolerate.

Even if you buy the Hard = Good equation, that's a tough sell. But you don't have a choice. Jesus isn't requesting your attendance at the Love Your Enemy Ball; he's telling you to do your level best to get there.

Do this: List your enemies on a sheet of paper. List anyone who has hurt you or is hurting you now, anyone whose indifference causes you pain.

Post the list where you'll see it often.

Then, at the top of that list, write this: My Prayer List.

Start praying, and see what happens in your world...and in you.

## AND EVEN GRITTIER

Share your list with another Jesus-follower. Ask that person to pray for you as you pray for the people on your list.

And—if you're really going for grit—invite your friend to ask you now and then how it's going.

How you're being transformed.

How you're becoming more like Jesus.

## TALK WITH JESUS

Jot your thoughts about...

- **What did you discover about yourself through these experiences?**

- **What did you learn about Jesus?**

- When you started praying, what if anything happened in your world...or in you?

- Where was the spiritual grit in these experiences? What strength have you gained that you didn't have before?

## GRIT GROWER 5: ENGAGE THE ENEMY

Maybe you've noticed: Things are tense these days.

Civil conversations are rare. Listening with the intent of understanding another person's point of view—that's pretty much on the endangered species list.

Which means it's easy to make enemies and demonize anyone who disagrees with you.

Do this: Think of an issue you're passionate about. It might be political, or it could be a moral stance you hold dear.

Whatever the issue, find someone on the other side of the fence and say, "I wonder if you'd help me understand why you see things the way you do."

Come with a sincere desire to understand, not debate. To accept, even if you don't endorse, what you hear.

And then listen until the person who's speaking feels understood.

Perhaps even loved.

# AND EVEN GRITTIER

Talk with a *family member* who's on the other side of an issue, someone with whom you've sparred in the past. Ask questions and listen to the answers.

Maybe it's atheist Uncle Jasper or the brother who thinks carrying a bazooka down Main Street is his God-given right. Any family member who holds an inflexible point of view that differs from yours is fair game.

Ask Jesus to use this experience to reframe what might be a contentious relationship with your family member.

And ask him for the grit to stay engaged in the conversation.

## TALK WITH JESUS

Jot your thoughts about...

- **What did you discover about yourself through these listening experiences?**

- **In what ways did your feelings about your "enemy" shift during your conversation...or didn't that happen?**

- **Where was the spiritual grit in these experiences? In what ways do you feel stronger?**

## GRIT GROWER 6: MAKE IT RIGHT

Sometimes people become your enemies, and it's not all their fault.

Sometimes you contribute, too.

And if that's the case, here's a grit-growing recommendation from Jesus:

"So if you are presenting a sacrifice at the altar in the Temple and you suddenly remember that someone has something against you, leave your sacrifice there at the altar. Go and be reconciled to that person. Then come and offer your sacrifice to God" (Matthew 5:23-24).

Actually, it's less a recommendation than an order.

To the extent you can make what's wrong between you and another person right, make it right.

Look at the prayer list (see Grit Grower 4) and pick a name. What, if anything, did you contribute to negatively affecting that relationship? And what, if anything, might you do to help fix what's broken?

Would an apology help? A more concrete action?

If you broke it, fix it. At least try.


## AND EVEN GRITTIER

Some say Jesus was just making a point when he said to settle differences before coming before God in worship. Others think he meant exactly what he said.

There's great grit in taking him literally on this one.

Before you show up at church or a Bible study again—before you finish this devotion—reach out to someone you've hurt and take a step toward making it right.

Meter's running.

## TALK WITH JESUS

Jot your thoughts about...

- **What did you discover about yourself through these experiences?**

- **What did you discover about Jesus?**

- **In what ways was this experience hard...and good?**

- **Where was the spiritual grit in these experiences? How would you describe yourself differently now, and why?**

# SERVE OTHERS

Jesus is the hottest ticket in town.

He shows up, and multitudes gather. Some come to be healed, some for a free meal, and others just to watch the show.

But show up they do—by the thousands. And right beside Jesus stand the disciples, basking in the applause washing over him.

It's heady stuff, and James and John, two fishermen used to long, lonely nights on the water, love it.

Perhaps a bit too much.

When their mother asks Jesus to give her boys favored spots in whatever new government he's creating, Jesus sees straight through her. He knows she's asking because her sons put her up to it.

What follows is a humbling, grit-building experience for James and John.

After telling them it's the Father's decision who'll be at his side, Jesus uses their request as a launching pad for a lesson on humility and servanthood.

Earthly rulers may lord their power over others, but that's not how things work in the kingdom of God. In Jesus' world, new rules apply.

"Whoever wants to be a leader among you must be your servant," Jesus says. "And whoever wants to be first among you must become your slave" (Matthew 20:26-27).

Gritty words for anyone grasping for position and power in Jesus' outfit. Both are available, Jesus says, but you won't get them by demanding them. And if you do end up at his side, many of the benefits most leaders enjoy will be missing.

You won't be served. You'll do the serving.

You won't be first in line. You'll be last.

And there's no room for whining because Jesus is doing the same thing he asks of you: to serve others.

"For even the Son of Man came not to be served but to serve others and give his life as a ransom for many," Jesus says (Matthew 20:28).*

Servanthood is the gravel pit of grit—it's humbling, hard, relentless, and all but impossible. What keeps Jesus' followers serving others is love—love for those they serve and the One they follow.

Any other motivation quickly wears thin.

Here's one way to know you're following Jesus: Your path is marked by opportunities to serve others.

How many of those opportunities are you seeing in your life?

And who are you serving?

We ask, not to shame you, but simply to raise the questions. Friends (can we call you a friend?) do that for each other: They ask prickly questions and have hard conversations because those are also ways to serve others.

So pause to consider your answers. They'll help you know if you're following Jesus or simply your notion of who Jesus might be.

What opportunities to serve are you seeing in life?

And who are you serving?

## GRIT GROWER 7: BAG IT AND TAG IT

Find a heavy-duty trash bag and a pair of work gloves.

All set?

Good—you're about to spend an hour serving people who aren't likely to thank you. And that's a hard-but-good thing for sure.

*Read the entire account in Matthew 20:20-28.*

Some won't notice what you're doing.

Others will notice but not care.

Either way, don't count on anyone aiming an appreciative "thumbs up" your way as you stroll through the neighborhood picking up trash that's settled on sidewalks, blown into doorways, and otherwise landed where nobody's likely to clean it up.

Which is what you're about to do.

A question to think about as you fill your bag with broken glass, discarded cans, and stray scraps of who-knows-what: How does it feel to serve when nobody appreciates you or your efforts?

Instead of expecting to be appreciated by those you're serving, look inward to Jesus: What is *he* saying to you?

## AND EVEN GRITTIER

Ratchet up your service: Adopt the route you just walked and do this again next week...and the week after.

See if this act of service becomes a habit.

See if anyone joins you.

And don't worry if nobody does.

## TALK WITH JESUS

Jot your thoughts about...

- **What did you discover about yourself through these experiences?**

- **How is what you've just done like and unlike what Jesus did?**

- In what ways was this experience hard...and good?

- Where was the spiritual grit in these experiences? How have they helped to develop your core strength?

## GRIT GROWER 8: HELP GRANDMA

Okay, not necessarily her.

But get ready to serve *someone* in your family—someone you can help in 15 minutes or less.

Maybe it's stepping in to do a chore that's on someone else's list, not yours. Quickly cleaning the kitchen because a parent dearly loves an uncluttered countertop.

Or giving Mom a foot rub. Or Dad a neck rub. Or maybe calling Grandma for a how-are-you-doing chat.

Ask Jesus who in your family would be encouraged by 15 minutes of selfless service, and what that service might be.

While you're at it, ask him this, too: How have you been serving me in ways I haven't noticed or appreciated? Listen for his voice. Then thank him.

## AND EVEN GRITTIER

Make the same offer to an elderly or infirm neighbor. Offer to do an hour of whatever needs to be done.

Be clear this isn't a request for a job; there's no bill coming.

If there's something on your neighbor's list you can't do (plumbing comes to mind), talk with other neighbors and recruit some help.

Serve...with no expectation of payment.

Serve as Jesus serves you.

Like the calluses forming on your fingers, you'll feel grit growing in your heart.

## TALK WITH JESUS

Jot your thoughts about...

- **What did you discover about yourself from these service experiences?**

- **What did you discover about Jesus?**

- **In what ways was this experience hard...and good?**

- **Where was the spiritual grit in these experiences? What's something you did that *required* the strength of Jesus to do, and why?**

## GRIT GROWER 9: LOOK FOR SOMEONE WHO'S STRUGGLING

This grit-building experience couldn't get much simpler.

It involves looking, then serving.

In the Bible, Jesus is always pausing to help someone. Run out of wine at a wedding celebration? Jesus helps out. Leprosy issue? Jesus to the rescue. Want to sort out a tricky theological issue? Jesus has your back.

Do the same today: Notice someone who's struggling and offer to help.

Maybe someone at school or work could use a word of encouragement.

Or down the street, someone may be struggling to clear a yard of leaves or a sidewalk of snow.

A person at the grocery store may be juggling way too many items and could use a helping hand or two.

Look around you today.

Look...notice...and serve.

## AND EVEN GRITTIER

Look deeper. Who's sad? Who's feeling the ache of loss? Who has fear etched on his face?

Serve by asking, "How are you? How are you *really*?"

Then listen...for as long as it takes.

## TALK WITH JESUS

Jot your thoughts about...

- **What did you discover about yourself as you looked and served?**

- **How was your serving like Jesus' expectations of his first disciples?**

- In what ways was this experience hard...and good?

- Where was the spiritual grit in these experiences? Jesus said when we serve "the least of these," we are actually serving him. How does that truth affect the way you serve?

# EXPECT THE UNEXPECTED

A crowd hikes into the wilderness to see Jesus. Thousands of people drop everything to see him.

Unfortunately, one thing they drop is a quick trip home to gather picnic supplies to carry with them.

Now they're here, dinnertime is approaching, and the disciples have pulled Jesus aside to suggest he send the crowd away to find food.

In response Jesus says, "*You* feed them."

Then Jesus goes back to what he was doing: healing, teaching, and most definitely *not* sending people away.

So...now what? Because *that* was totally unexpected.

Jesus has given his dozen closest disciples the ability to cast out demons and heal illnesses. But rustling up dinner for more than 5,000 people? They're clueless.

There's not enough money to buy food. Besides, where could they find a bakery that could bag up enough bagels to satisfy this crowd?

Still, Jesus is expecting them to do *something*...

Andrew finds a young man who's carrying five barley loaves and two small fish. The Bible doesn't describe how Andrew knows the kid's packing a snack. Maybe the disciples fanned out asking for donations, and this guy was the only one dumb enough to raise his hand and risk losing what little he brought with him.

However he was outed, the young man is hustled straight to Jesus.

You know what happens next: Jesus multiplies the meal until there's enough fish sandwiches for everyone—with 12 baskets of leftovers to haul home.*

Jesus could have made things easier for his disciples. He could have simply prayed a catered lunch into existence—but that's not what he chooses to do.

Instead, he hands them a how-do-I-solve-this challenge and tells them to act. When they do, he multiplies and blesses what they accomplish, no matter how meager the fruit of their labors.

And that's how grit grows. Jesus asks, we do, and then we see what he does with the little we bring to him.

And an annoyingly large percentage of Jesus' requests come as surprises.

Someone with whom you have a fractured relationship ends up sitting next to you in class, and you have no excuse for not talking. You come into a sudden pile of unexpected money (hey, it *could* happen), and you're forced to decide: Spend it on yourself or others?

If you're following Jesus, expect the unexpected. It's coming. It's how he rolls.

Yes, Jesus could have solved the disciples' problem for them, but grit doesn't grow on the path of least resistance or easy answers.

For them, for you, it's found far more often where there's no choice but to do your best and turn to Jesus for help.

## GRIT GROWER 10: TEMPORARY LEFTY...OR RIGHTY

Sometimes it's easier to see Jesus when you step outside your routines, even a little.

Do this: Get ready for your day using your nondominant hand. If you're a righty, brush your teeth with your left hand.

Lefty? Button and zip up your clothes with your right hand.

Allow extra time, by the way; tying your shoes is going to take some doing.

*Read the entire account in Matthew 14:13-21.

As you feel your patience grow thin, as you struggle with tasks you can usually do on automatic pilot, notice the unexpected—maybe unwelcome—surprises that show up.

Ask yourself: In what ways is what you're experiencing like following Jesus?

And how do you typically react to the challenging surprises he tosses your way?

## AND EVEN GRITTIER

It's hard to plan your own surprises, so you'll need some help.

Call a friend and ask for her help with a quick project at your place. Twenty minutes, tops.

When your friend arrives, ask her to rearrange the furniture in your room. She's to move every stick of furniture somehow. Drag the bed over here, place the lamp over there—you get the idea.

Meanwhile, you'll wait in another room as your friend redecorates.

Live with the new furniture placement for at least a week. See how long it takes you to get accustomed to what was a *substantial* surprise when you first walked into the room.

A word of advice: Leave a lamp burning at night. Should you walk through the room in the dark, your toes will get a sharp reminder that the dresser has migrated.

## TALK WITH JESUS

Jot your thoughts about...

- **What did you discover about yourself as you coped with surprises?**


- **How was this like what the first disciples experienced in their lives?**

- In what ways was this experience hard...and good?


- Where was the spiritual grit in these experiences? In what ways have you depended more on Jesus as a result of these surprises?


## GRIT GROWER 11: THAT OTHER CHANNEL

You have approximately a zillion channels available on your TV and a bazillion more on your laptop or tablet, but you probably watch less than a dozen with any regularity.

Not today.

Pick a channel at random—one you never select—and watch for half an hour. Expose yourself to something new and surprising (but not something you have to repent of later). Look for anything that reminds you of Jesus.

You'll be surprised what leaps out at you.

Surprise!


## AND EVEN GRITTIER

Call that friend from the "Even Grittier" section of Grit Grower 10 and explain you'd like to take her to a movie.

Your treat...sort of.

Pick a time, and together, head to the local multiplex. When you get to the box office, buy tickets to the next movie that's showing—even if you've never heard of it. Even if you've heard of it and thought, "There's no way I'd sit through *that*."

Buy two tickets, hand one to your brave friend, and rustle up a bucket of popcorn to share.

Then find two seats and settle in.

Afterward, talk with your friend about the film and how this was like dealing with surprises that pop up in life. How sometimes doing unexpected things gets you ready for other unexpected things. How grit is worth growing.

You're going to have a *great* conversation.

## TALK WITH JESUS

Jot your thoughts about...

- **What did you discover about yourself as you went through these experiences?**

- **How was this like dealing with surprises that Jesus lets come into your life—especially those that show up because you're following him?**

- **In what ways was this experience hard...and good?**

- **Where was the spiritual grit in these experiences? How does inviting risk into your relationship with Jesus draw you closer to him?**

# OBEY JESUS

Obedience.

*There's* a word not likely to be voted Most Likely to Succeed.

If you've ever lived with a 2-year-old, you know we're not wired for obedience. We have opinions we want noted, preferences we expect to be respected.

And whether or not we say it aloud, we're pretty sure our way is the best way.

Jesus' first disciples were a lot like us in that regard, so it's likely they were less than thrilled when Jesus said, "If you love me, obey my commandments" (John 14:15).*

Just...obey, no questions asked?

Meaning Jesus won't put all major decisions to a vote? Really?

Jesus sets obedience as a quick, no-compromise bar he expects anyone following him to clear.

Um...just who does this Jesus character think he *is*?

And there—right there—is the heart of the matter.

Jesus can demand obedience precisely *because* of who he is: Savior. Lord. Master. God.

He doesn't owe anyone a rationale or explanation. He doesn't have to cajole or convince. He's in charge; the kingdom of God isn't a democracy.

His followers don't get a vote; they just get to decide if they love him.

If they love him, they'll follow him.

*Read the entire account in John 14:15-21.

And if they follow him, they'll obey.

This is gritty stuff made all the grittier because we tend to hear the word *obey* as a harsh command. It's what annoyed parents say to disobedient children. It's all about establishing who's in charge.

But Jesus doesn't insist on obedience just to flex his muscles. He's ever and always about love. He obeys the Father (John 6:38) because of love, and he expects you and the rest of his followers to obey him for the same reason.

Because you love him.

For Jesus, obedience is all about the heart, not just behavior.

So maybe *obey* isn't a four-letter word after all. At least, not a distasteful one.

Jesus' expectation of obedience is an opportunity rather than a mean-spirited demand.

An opportunity to reap the benefits of abiding in him.

An opportunity to have an even closer friendship with him.

An opportunity to grow grit.

## GRIT GROWER 12: OBEY THE RULES

Make that obey *all* the rules—including the ones you usually ignore. Even the dumb rules that make no sense to you.

Driving? Stay under every posted speed limit. Stop fully at every stop sign. Toss your cellphone in the trunk so you won't be tempted to check for texts.

Working at a fast-food joint? Make sure your break lasts exactly as long as it's supposed to. Clean the back line the way your manager showed you.

Doing homework? Check your grammar and spelling as if your life depended on it. Follow every grammar rule.

Wash your hands when the health department expects you to. Stick to a healthy diet. Read all the instructions before beginning.

In short, become a poster child for the Keep the Rules Foundation.

All the rules. All day. No exceptions.

# AND EVEN GRITTIER

*Disobey* all the rules—and see what happens.

Well, maybe not *all* the rules...but those that won't get you killed or arrested if you disobey them.

See how far you get today before your life gets very, very complicated.

Ask yourself as you go: Which is the better way to care for myself and others, through obedience or disobedience?

How does each stance affect your relationship with Jesus?

## TALK WITH JESUS

Jot your thoughts about...

- **What did you discover about yourself as you explored obedience?**

- **How was your attitude toward obeying *all* the rules like or unlike your attitude toward obeying Jesus?**

- **In what ways was this experience hard...and good?**

- **Where was the spiritual grit in these experiences? How is a growing capacity for obedience related to your level of spiritual grit?**

Give yourself an assignment. Order yourself to bake a cake...change your car's oil...write a sonnet.

Anything that you have no idea how to do.

Now find an online tutorial and figure out how to obey the order you gave yourself.

As you charge into unknown territory, you're obeying—but it's energizing, isn't it? Even if you fail, you're fully engaged, alive, and focused.

How is that like obeying Jesus?

## AND EVEN GRITTIER

You're going to need to borrow a pet—yours or a friend's. A friendly one.

Your goal: to train an old dog (or cat or hamster) to do a new trick. It can be roll over, play dead, or drive a stick shift—whatever you decide.

Just be sure the pet doesn't already know the trick. That's cheating.

Use whatever treats and techniques you think will best convince the pet to listen to you and obey the command.

Give yourself 30 minutes; then see how the pet performs.

It doesn't count if the pet intends to obey but doesn't get around to it. Or if Fido explains that what you've asked isn't convenient or in his area of giftedness.

The pet either will or won't obey your command.

It will happen...or it won't.

So give this a try...and as you do, ask yourself this: In what ways is what you're doing like and unlike what Jesus does with you?

And in what ways are you like or unlike Fido?

# TALK WITH JESUS

Jot your thoughts about...

- What did you discover about yourself as you went through these experiences? And how about the pet? Did it learn anything?

- What did you discover about obedience and how Jesus goes about helping you obey him?

- In what ways was this experience hard...and good?

- Where was the spiritual grit in these experiences? We often think if we knew exactly what Jesus wanted us to do, we'd do it, but that's not always true. Why do we disobey even when we know what Jesus wants?

## GRIT GROWER 14: OBEDIENCE REVIEW

Go to a river, lake, or pond where you can toss rocks into the water without creating a problem.

(Swimming pools are out. Let's get that straight at the get-go.)

Take a pocketful of pebbles or pennies with you. Anything you can toss in the water and not miss later.

As you stand next to the water, think of ways you haven't obeyed Jesus.

Things you've done. Things you've left undone. Things you've said or thought. With each memory of a disobedient moment, toss one of your pebbles into the water and watch it disappear from sight.

This may take awhile.

When you've finished—or run out of pebbles—tell Jesus you're sorry. Ask for his help as you move forward in your gritty, stop-and-start discipleship journey.

You've just repented, and Jesus is faithful to forgive, so let those memories of disobedience disappear under the water just as the pebbles did.

Instead of looking over your shoulder, look ahead.

At a life of transformation. Of growing in your friendship with Jesus. Of obedience, not because you have to, but because you want to honor your Friend.

## AND EVEN GRITTIER

Add a second pocketful of pebbles and repeat this activity—this time choosing to forgive the people who've disobeyed you.

Classmates who dropped the ball on team projects and left you holding the bag for finishing a group project. Friends whose follow-through left you disappointed.

Forgive their disobedience as Jesus has forgiven yours.

## TALK WITH JESUS

Jot your thoughts about...

- **What did you discover about yourself as you considered those times you and others have been less than obedient?**

- How did it feel to confess...and repent...and be forgiven?

- In what ways was this experience hard...and good?

- Where was the spiritual grit in these experiences? Why does it require so much strength to be humble and vulnerable?

# FORGIVE THEM ANYWAY

It's hard enough to forgive friends who accidentally hurt you, friends who apologize when they realize what they've done.

But forgiving people who *purposely* hurt you or someone you love? And then don't care about what they've done?

That's hard. *That* takes spiritual grit.

It takes the sort of grit Jesus shows when, from the cross, he prays, "Father, forgive them, for they don't know what they are doing" (Luke 23:34).

Sorry to disagree, Jesus, but the religious leaders smirking in the distance and those soldiers rolling dice to see who wins your robe know *exactly* what they're doing: They're killing you.

Slowly.

Intentionally.

And they'll sleep just fine tonight.

What they don't understand is the significance of their actions. They don't know who they've nailed to that cross.

But even with the sound of their laughter ringing in your ears, you forgive them. And you ask God to do the same.*

That's the standard Jesus sets when it comes to forgiveness: Do it anyway...even if the people hammering spikes through your hands aren't the least bit sorry. Even if they think they're doing God a favor by murdering you.

That's the gritty kind of forgiveness Jesus expects from his disciples—then and now.

*Read the entire account in Luke 23:26-38.

He makes it even more impossible by saying this: "If you forgive those who sin against you, your heavenly Father will forgive you. But if you refuse to forgive others, your Father will not forgive your sins" (Matthew 6:14-15).

Oh, great. Now flunking Forgiveness 101 means you don't get forgiven yourself.

This just gets better and better...

But here's the thing: While you can't muster up the grit to forgive on your own, with Jesus' help, it's possible.

It fact, it's *only* possible with Jesus' help.

On your own you can find a way to excuse bad behavior or repress the memory of what someone has done to you or a loved one. There's evil in the world, people are broken, abusers were abused—you know the drill.

But forgiveness—deep, lasting, soul-soothing forgiveness— that's the stuff of heaven. And that takes the help of Someone who's been there.

Who, if anyone, needs your forgiveness—whether that person knows it or not?

And what, if anything, are you willing to do about it?

## GRIT GROWER 15: SLOW FADE TO FORGIVENESS

Head to the dollar store, and buy a helium balloon. Take a permanent marker with you, or pick one up while you're balloon shopping.

The balloon's design doesn't matter, but get one that's colorful and easy to see.

Take your balloon to an open field or parking lot—somewhere your view isn't blocked by trees or buildings.

Using the marker, write something you've found hard to forgive on the balloon. Be specific, but don't name names.

Invite Jesus to join you as you release the balloon. Ask him to stand beside you as the two of you watch it grow smaller, then smaller still, and then disappear altogether.

As you watch, ask Jesus this question: *How can you help the pain I feel fade away in the same way the balloon is fading into the distance?*

Listen carefully. The answer may require grit, but it will bring healing.

## AND EVEN GRITTIER

Write on your balloon, but don't release it.

Instead, carry it home, and tie it where others can see it. How does it feel to have the thing that's hard to forgive out in the open? In what ways do you feel more, or less, free because it's out in the open?

## TALK WITH JESUS

Jot your thoughts about...

- **What did you discover about yourself as you talked with Jesus about forgiveness?**

- **What did you discover about Jesus as the two of you watched the balloon disappear?**

- **In what ways was this experience hard...and good?**

- Where was the spiritual grit in these experiences? What new strength have you noticed in yourself as a result of these experiences?

## GRIT GROWER 16: FORGIVING...YESTERDAY

Forgiving others isn't something to put off.

If you hang onto a hurt too long, it may become almost impossible to let go. It becomes part of you, a piece of your story that defines you.

So do this: Think about yesterday.

In fact, pull out your calendar now or fire up your laptop to scheduling software that will walk you through the past 24 hours or so.

What happened yesterday that you could forgive now, rather than letting it simmer?

And in what way, if any, did you have a hand in those hard situations?

Maybe your words escalated a conflict rather than calmed it. Maybe your attitude sparked a fire or fanned the flames of an already heated moment.

Ask Jesus to help you remember and then do more than remember: forgive.

## AND EVEN GRITTIER

Have the conversation with Jesus as you're tackling that cleaning chore you've put off because you hate it.

Maybe your room would give the health department hives. Or you could plant corn in the carpet of your car and it would sprout. Or the dust bunnies under your bed are the size of dust buffaloes.

Ask Jesus to give you insight as you clean: How is leaving forgiveness for later like what happens when you leave cleaning for later?

# TALK WITH JESUS

Jot your thoughts about...

- **What did you discover about yourself as you considered forgiving others and yourself?**

- **How does deciding to forgive remind you of Jesus? And of his friendship with you?**

- **In what ways was this experience hard...and good?**

- **Where was the spiritual grit in these experiences? Why, exactly, do we often put off doing hard things?**

## GRIT GROWER 17: FORGIVENESS FLOWERS

Give a bouquet of flowers to someone you need to forgive. Something sunny and bright. Daisies, maybe.

Don't specify on the accompanying card why you're giving flowers; just sign the card and let that be enough.

Once you've tucked the receipt in your pocket or purse, reflect on this: How does it feel to invest in a failed or fractured relationship?

What will you say if the person on the receiving end of the bouquet asks you why?

# AND EVEN GRITTIER

Same say-it-with-flowers activity.

Same investment made in a relationship that's on life support.

Probably best not to give flowers a second time to someone you need to forgive, but if you can't think of at least one other person who's hurt you, you're not trying.

This time, though, consider this: What will you say to Jesus—and yourself—if the person never says anything to you about your gift?

## TALK WITH JESUS

Jot your thoughts about...

- **What did you discover about yourself as you gave flowers to someone who's wronged you?**

- **How is what you've done for that person like what Jesus has done for you?**

- **In what ways was this experience hard...and good?**

- **Where was the spiritual grit in these experiences? How is what you did like what Jesus does with you every day?**

# EMBRACE TRANSFORMATION...
# EVEN IF IT HURTS

Jesus' first disciples knew how to please God:
1) Learn the rules.
2) Obey the rules.
3) Repeat.
Toss in an occasional sacrificial lamb to smooth over the times rules were bent or broken, and everything's kosher.

It's the system Jesus' first disciples were taught in synagogue. It's what all the rabbis preached. As a system for making God happy, it's clear, clean, and predictable.

And then Jesus upsets everything, saying, "You have heard that our ancestors were told, 'You must not murder. If you commit murder, you are subject to judgment.'

"But I say, if you are even angry with someone, you are subject to judgment! If you call someone an idiot, you are in danger of being brought before the court. And if you curse someone, you are in danger of the fires of hell."*

That's when the disciples swallow hard and make a mental note: *We're gonna need a lot more sacrificial lambs*.

That God cares about more than their actions wasn't news— that message was hammered home throughout the psalms and the prophets. But because looking solely at actions is easy, that's where many religious leaders in Jesus' day landed.

*Read the entire account in Matthew 5:21-26.*

Not Jesus, though.

He's after more than compliance.

He wants to see *transformation,* and that goes far deeper than just doing things. It's change from the inside out—and that both takes and builds spiritual grit.

It happens when we abide in Jesus, relying on him instead of ourselves, our circumstances, or others.

Jesus calls his followers to do more than just modify their outward behavior. He declares that, moving forward, their thoughts and motives are up for review, too.

And what was true for them is true for you, too.

So how does the notion that Jesus knows your thoughts and motivations strike you? Is being so well known by him a comfort...or something else?

Why?

## GRIT GROWER 18: MARK YOUR GROWTH

Remember when you were a little kid and your year-to-year growth was tracked by pencil marks on a doorjamb or pantry door?

You'd stand there in your bare feet, someone would lay a ruler on your head, and yet another line would appear that declared you were growing.

Growth as a disciple isn't measured in pencil marks. It's measured in transformation, in a changed heart and faithful living.

But that doesn't mean you can't pull out a ruler and pencil anyway.

Stand against a doorjamb and ask someone to mark your height with a pencil line. Then ask Jesus how you've been growing as a disciple. Compared to a year ago, where's transformation happening in your life?

## AND EVEN GRITTIER

Invite someone who knows you well to be the one who makes the pencil mark; then risk asking, *How do you see transformation happening in my life? In what ways am I different from the person I was a year or two ago?*

That's a tough question, so give your friend time to consider his or her answer.

It's tough because the transformation may be internal and gradual, not yet visible from the outside.

It's tough because perhaps the transformation is subtle, something only you've noticed.

And it's tough because your friend might honestly not see any transformation in you—just your circumstances. And that's a hard message to deliver.

So ask, wait, and see what Jesus does with the conversation.

## TALK WITH JESUS

Jot your thoughts about...

- **What did you discover about yourself as you talked with your friend about transformation?**

- **In what ways are you being transformed by your relationship with Jesus?**

- **In what ways was this experience hard...and good?**

- Where was the spiritual grit in these experiences? What's usually true about your transforming experiences?

## GRIT GROWER 19: EMBRACE HUMILITY

It's tough to be transformed until you're ready to change.

And it's tough to change until you admit that, just maybe, you don't know everything and you don't have it all together. And *that* is a grit-growing admission.

See where this is headed?

Do this: Try something and fail. Fail big. Fail in a way that leaves no doubt that you're failing. Here's how...

Get a half-dozen small balls, empty plastic soda bottles, or hacky sacks, and in the privacy of your home, try juggling.

If you're like most non-jugglers, this won't go well. Prepare to be humbled.

The truth is, while juggling doesn't look all that hard, to be transformed into a capable juggler, you need help. Coaching. Someone to show you the ropes and help you practice.

Until then you're probably just one more person chasing rubber balls around the room.

## AND EVEN GRITTIER

Gather up your juggling supplies, and find a spot people can see you. A subway or bus stop. Outside the door of a grocery store. Anywhere you're out of the way but still in the spotlight.

And fail there.

If someone who actually knows how to juggle has mercy on you and offers a quick tutorial, humbly accept the help.

Transformation often travels hand in hand with humility. So be humble.

And if you already know how to juggle, pick another activity. Singing opera comes to mind.

## TALK WITH JESUS

Jot your thoughts about...

- What did you discover about yourself and humility? Would people who know you well say you're a humble person? Why or why not?

- How does Jesus model humility? What has that meant to you?

- In what ways was this experience hard...and good?

- Where was the spiritual grit in these experiences? What exactly makes humility hard for you sometimes? What makes it easy?

## GRIT GROWER 20: MAKE SPACE

Jesus didn't settle for wedging himself into the regular routines of his first disciples.

He insisted they clear their calendars and be with him around the clock, soaking up what he said, how he lived, what he valued.

He demanded focused attention, something we current disciples are very, very bad at giving him.

Until now.

Because now—or as soon as you can arrange it—you'll unplug for 24 hours.

That means no video games, television, or media of any kind that's not absolutely required for you to stay in school or employed.

Instead, use that time to make space for transformation. For thinking about Jesus. For listening for his voice.

For just one day, don't expect him to shout over your distractions.

Focus on him instead.

Invite transformation.

## AND EVEN GRITTIER

Add fasting to your 24 hours of focused attention on Jesus.

This spiritual discipline is more than simply not eating. It's setting aside food so you can sharpen your focus on Jesus.

Take the usual precautions—drink lots of water and be sure medications that are to be taken with food can safely be consumed.

Then commit to a prayerful, focused, media-free, 24-hour fast as you make space for Jesus to nudge your transformation forward.

## TALK WITH JESUS

Jot your thoughts about...

- **What happened during your 24 hours of focused attention on Jesus?**

- What did you discover about Jesus? about yourself?

- In what ways was this experience hard...and good?

- Where was the spiritual grit in these experiences? Somewhere along the line, your ability to persevere was tested. How did that affect your relationship with Jesus?

# JUDGE CAREFULLY

It's exactly the sort of thing that raises the disciples' blood pressure—and it happens all the time.

It seems every time they turn around someone's interrupting Jesus. Demanding his attention. Delaying him on his way to somewhere important.

This time it's a woman who shows up at a dinner party.

Nobody notices her as she comes in—Simon of Bethany is hosting Jesus and the disciples in his home, and they're busy talking and eating. But she makes her way over to Jesus and pours expensive perfume over his head.

A nice gesture, but not every disciple approves.

Some of them throw up their hands in exasperation. Why didn't the woman donate the perfume instead? It's expensive—*astoundingly* expensive—and could have been sold to provide money for the poor. It's just this kind of short-sighted theatrics that...

Jesus rises to the blushing woman's defense, quieting his complaining disciples with a command and a question. "Leave her alone," he says. "Why criticize her for doing such a good thing to me? You will always have the poor among you, and you can help them whenever you want to. But you will not always have me" (Mark 14:6-7).

The disciples have misjudged both the woman and Jesus.

She wasn't being wasteful; she was worshipping.

And Jesus wasn't counting costs; he was counting down the days until his body would be anointed again, this time for burial.

The disciples have forgotten what Jesus said earlier about judging others:

"Do not judge others, and you will not be judged. For you will be treated as you treat others. The standard you use in judging is the standard by which you will be judged" (Matthew 7:1-2).

Jesus isn't suggesting that you and the rest of his followers never judge situations or people. He's simply saying that the standards you use to pass judgment may well be applied to you.

Which is about the most powerful motivation to develop restraint that Jesus could possibly trot out for his followers.*

If you're quick to judge, expect the same. If you always assume a negative motivation for others' actions, that's a standard you might see applied to yourself.

How do you feel, knowing that Jesus reserves the right to judge you using the same standards you use to judge others?

Happy thought...or something else?

## GRIT GROWER 21: PEOPLE-WATCHING

Find a spot that's good for people-watching.

A public park. The zoo. A bench at the mall.

Then do this: Decide which people you're drawn to and which you aren't. Two lists—people you'd welcome if they were to sit down next to you and those who, as far as you're concerned, can keep on walking.

Mentally sort passersby for five or ten minutes.

Then ask yourself: *How did I decide who's in each group? How did I pass judgment?*

Jot your thoughts in the margins of this page. You won't be describing how you think you *should* judge others; you'll describe how you *actually* judge others.

And no matter how uncomfortable the thought, you do judge others. We all do.

*Read the entire account in Mark 14:1-9.

GROWING SPIRITUAL GRIT
FOR TEENAGERS

Review what you wrote. What sort of picture do your comments paint? Is it a portrait of a person who's caring? curious? open—or closed?

And how comfortable are you with others judging you in the same way you've judged them?

## AND EVEN GRITTIER

Being called judgmental is one of the ultimate insults of our time.

But risk it: Invite another Jesus-follower to join you at the mall.

Do the people-watching described previously, but quietly compare notes—about who ends up on your lists and why.

Then, together, read Matthew 7:1-2 and grapple with Jesus' words. If he's serious, what does that mean about how the two of you live your daily lives? What, if anything, do you want to change? What would it take to make those changes?

---

*"Do not judge others, and you will not be judged. For you will be treated as you treat others. The standard you use in judging is the standard by which you will be judged" (Matthew 7:1-2).*

---

## TALK WITH JESUS

Jot your thoughts about...

- **What did you discover about yourself through these judging experiences?**


- **What did you discover about Jesus?**

- In what ways was this experience hard...and good?



- Where was the spiritual grit in these experiences? What are the pros and cons of self-knowledge?


## GRIT GROWER 22: A QUESTION FOR YOU, OFFICER...

You know a police officer, right?

No? Ask around—someone you know does. Get a name and an introduction.

Police officers make judgment calls all day long.

Who's a threat and who isn't.

Who's dangerous and who's just distracted or angry.

Who to pull over, who to ticket, and who to let off with a warning.

Police officers' ability to make quick judgments can save lives—theirs and yours.

Do this: Ask an officer (either in person or via email) how he or she makes decisions. What factors play into deciding if there's a problem? What signals cause that officer to move closer for a better look?

See what you can learn—good and bad—about judging others.

### AND EVEN GRITTIER

Call your local police station and ask if you (or you and a Jesus-following friend) can ride along in a patrol car.

Some departments allow this; some don't. You won't know unless you ask.

While in the squad car, observe how the officer makes decisions. Ask what that officer has learned over the years that's sharpened an ability to make quick, on-target judgments.

Be respectful...and pay attention. You're seeing experience in action.

You might even be seeing spiritual grit.

## TALK WITH JESUS

Jot your thoughts about...

- **What did you discover about yourself during these experiences?**




- **What did you discover about passing judgment?**




- **In what ways was this experience hard...and good?**




- **Where was the spiritual grit in these experiences? Why is it so easy to judge others harshly and so hard to judge them fairly?**

# BE ALL-IN

Jesus and his 12 closest followers are together, celebrating the Passover meal in a cozy, lamp-lit room. Jesus has been distracted all evening; there's clearly something weighing heavily on his mind.

And then Jesus says this: "I am the way, the truth, and the life. No one can come to the Father except through me" (John 14:6).

The disciples trade nervous glances because that kind of talk can get you in trouble. *Serious* trouble.

The disciples have heard Jesus say things like this before, but not while they were sitting in Jerusalem. Not where a curious eavesdropper might hear Jesus' words and carry them straight across town to a high priest looking for any excuse to charge Jesus with blasphemy.

Or worse, that same someone might tell the Romans.

Romans ruled a vast empire, so they'd adopted a live-and-let-live approach to religion. You could believe in whatever local gods you wanted, as long as you also acknowledged *their* gods.

Which is exactly what Jesus isn't doing.

He's declaring that he's *it.* Forget Jupiter and Juno; Jesus is tossing Roman deities out like so many rotten figs.

Jesus is saying to believe in him—and *only* him. There's no room for splitting your allegiance or hedging your bets. Either you're all-in with him, or you're looking in the wrong place.

Which is a very, very dangerous thing to say.

If Jesus is serious—and the disciples can see he is—he's announcing yet again that they have a choice: They can be all-in with him...or not. There's no middle ground.

What they *can't* be is lukewarm about him, and neither can anyone else.

So in that shadowed room, two unspoken questions hang in the air:

Do the disciples believe Jesus is who he says he is...or not?

And what are they willing to do about it?*

Those same two questions wait for anyone—like you—who's following Jesus. They slice the cloth right down the middle, and you're on one side or the other.

If you believe in Jesus, that's fine, but it's nothing special. Lots of people believe in Jesus. It's easy to do that. Comforting and inspirational, even.

But believing that Jesus is who he says he is? That he's *the* way, *the* truth, and *the* life, and nobody comes to the Father except through him?

That's the harder question.

So for you, the same two questions that floated through the minds of 12 people seated around a low table with Jesus:

*Do I believe Jesus is who he says he is...or not?*

*And what am I willing to do about it?*

Answer carefully. There's a wealth of grit to be mined in those decisions.

## GRIT GROWER 23: TUB TIME

It's time to be all-in...your bathtub.

So do this: Fill your tub with warm water. Place a fluffy towel nearby. Add bubbles and light a candle, if you're so inclined. Play some relaxing music.

Do your level best to transform your bathroom into a five-star spa.

Then slide into the warm, inviting water—without disturbing it. Without making a splash or prompting a ripple.

If possible without even raising the water level.

*Read the entire account in John 14:6-14.

Try as you might, you can't do it. When you're all-in a bathtub, it shows.

It's the same with Jesus. If you're all-in, it shows in what you say, how you live, and how you describe him to others.

As you soak, talk with Jesus about how you're doing with being all-in. Does he see you that way? If not, what does he want you to do about it?

## AND EVEN GRITTIER

Still in the tub?

Good. Stay there.

Stay there as the warm water grows tepid, then cool, then uncomfortably cold.

Don't move as you think about this: How willing are you to be all-in with Jesus when things get hard?

Pray for grit—because challenging, chilly times are coming.

Oh, and climb on out of there and towel off. You'll catch your death of cold.

## TALK WITH JESUS

Jot your thoughts about...

- **Other than how much you needed a relaxing bath, what did you discover about yourself through these experiences?**

- **What did you hear from Jesus? What, if anything, did he say to you?**

- In what ways was this experience hard...and good?

- Where was the spiritual grit in these experiences? How does an all-in attitude affect your ability to persevere through hard things?

## GRIT GROWER 24: ALL-IN FOR A LONG TIME

A friendship with Jesus is a lot like marriage.

Both relationships take commitment. Passion. An expectation the relationship will go the distance.

Do this: Find a couple who's been married a long time and ask if you can talk with them about why, in a world where so many marriages fail, theirs has lasted.

Here are some questions you might ask:

- What do you do as a couple that protects your marriage?
- What is most challenging about an all-in marriage?
- What's helped you weather the hard times in your marriage?
- What advice would you give younger couples who want their marriages to thrive?

Take notes—this is grit served up on a platter.

And remember to send a thank-you card.

## AND EVEN GRITTIER

Maybe the idea of being passionately committed to Jesus feels...awkward.

Committed, yes. But passionate?

That's just creepy.

Except if you're *not* passionate, if you don't take your commitment to Jesus at least as seriously as you take wedding vows, you won't stick with him. You'll wander away and not come back.

Do this: Invite a few Jesus-followers to join you for a public commitment to Jesus. Even if you've been confirmed, dedicated, baptized, and born again, read the following aloud, in public, where witnesses see and hear you. It's a reminder to you and a statement to the world: When it comes to Jesus, you're all-in.

"Jesus, I, [your name], promise to love, honor, and obey you. I will abide in you in sickness and in health, for richer or for poorer, as long as I live. I trust in you alone as my Savior and Lord."

You may now cut the cake and serve it to your witnesses.

## TALK WITH JESUS

Jot your thoughts about...

- **What did you discover about being all-in and committed from these experiences?**

- **What did you learn about yourself?**

- **In what ways was this experience hard...and good?**

- **Where was the spiritual grit in these experiences? When has it really cost you to follow Jesus, and why did you pay the price?**

Your life can get busy. Probably *does* get busy, as you're pushed and pulled in different directions by people and projects you could or should get done.

So you set priorities. Well, you set them or discover that other people are setting them for you.

Today you'll pick a third option. You'll invite Jesus to set your priorities for you.

But go into this with your eyes open: Asking Jesus to take charge is a guaranteed jump into grit territory. He may take you to unexpected places, steer you in a new direction.

Do it anyway.

Ask Jesus to set your priorities and agenda for the next 24 hours. Your tasks, school work, social calendar, entertainment—the whole enchilada.

Ask...then listen.

Listen...then do.

That's being all-in.

## AND EVEN GRITTIER

Put your wallet or purse on the table, too.

During the next 24 hours, invite Jesus to speak into how you spend your money as well as your time.

## TALK WITH JESUS

Jot your thoughts about...

- **What did you discover about yourself when you allowed Jesus to tell you how to use your time and resources for a day?**

- What did you discover about Jesus and what he values?

- In what ways was this experience hard...and good?

- Where was the spiritual grit in these experiences? What did you discover about Jesus as you moved through these experiences?

# GET USED TO UNCOMFORTABLE

Jesus' dozen disciples are excited.

They've watched Jesus heal lepers and cast out demons, but always from the sidelines. Now he's pulled them together for a chat before he sends them out to do what they've seen him do.

This is big stuff. This is where they make Jesus proud.

Jesus has outlined the mission. Covered the logistics. Communicated the importance of what they'll be doing and why they're doing it.

And now there's nervous energy crackling around the room as Jesus waits for his followers to quiet down. Then, as they hang on to every word, he says this:

"You will be handed over to the courts and will be flogged with whips in the synagogues. You will stand trial before governors and kings because you are my followers...all nations will hate you because you are my followers...Don't be afraid of those who want to kill your body" (Matthew 10:17-18, 22, 28).

As pep talks go, it's a bit of a letdown.[*]

But it's Jesus' honest take on what's coming. If you're following him, you'd best grow some grit because—like it or not—things will get hard.

As in hate-you, hurt-you, drag-you-into-court hard.

*Read the entire account in Matthew 10:5-42.

Jesus doesn't sugarcoat the cost of following him. If you pursue the kingdom of God with anything approaching passion, you'll collide with the culture around you.

Your values won't align with those of many of the people in your life.

You'll march to the beat of a drummer some people can't—or won't—hear.

You'll encounter conflict, and there's no guarantee Jesus will do anything to sand those rough edges off your life. In fact, he may choose to do just the *opposite*. He may leave them there, snagging you at every turn.

Uncomfortable may well become your new normal.

Does Jesus care that you're experiencing discomfort? Sure. If you're like most people, you measure his friendship in part by whether he does something to cause hard stuff to stop.

That's what friends do, right? They remember your birthday. They make sympathetic noises when you're sad.

Friends are supposed to be people who make our lives easier. People who see us wince and offer a backrub.

So why does Jesus claim to be your friend and then announce that hanging around with him will usher no end of hard stuff into your life? Hard stuff that he apparently has no intention of shielding you from?

From his perspective, the hard you encounter is often good. It drives you to him, causes you to rely on him. It's fertile soil for growing spiritual grit.

Yes, there's rough water ahead—you can count on it. But take heart in knowing this: You're not navigating it alone.

Your friend Jesus is with you.

If it's true that following Jesus positions you to experience conflict with your culture—what does it say if you're *not* experiencing conflict?

If your journey is smooth and seamless?

When's the last time your allegiance to Jesus caused you to bump up against conflict? And what might it mean if that's not happening?

## GRIT GROWER 26: FINISHING

When things get uncomfortable, it's easy to think that's a signal to move along, to find a path with fewer obstacles in your way.

But remember: When you follow Jesus, "hard" is often just another way to say "good."

So find something you stopped doing because it was hard, and finish it.

The essay you started but decided to put off.

The daily run that turned into a weekly run that turned into "what run?"

The friendship you let die of neglect because it required forgiveness.

Go finish something hard. Something that takes grit to bring in for a landing.

## AND EVEN GRITTIER

Finishing something builds grit.

Finishing something for someone else, something that takes considerable effort, drops a shovel full of grit into your life.

What's something that someone in your life can't do?

Pulling leaves out of a gutter, moving a refrigerator so you can give the kitchen floor under it a good cleaning—anything that puts you at the intersection of Listening to Jesus and Uncomfortable.

That's where you're headed.

So go volunteer.

Let Jesus build some grit in your life.

# TALK WITH JESUS

Jot your thoughts about...

- **What are you discovering about yourself as you struggle with finishing something—for yourself or someone else?**

- **What are you discovering about Jesus?**

- **In what ways was this experience hard...and good?**

- **Where was the spiritual grit in these experiences? What's the difference between people who quit halfway through a challenge and those who don't?**

## GRIT GROWER 27: HUGS

Make a large sign that says, "Free hugs."
Go stand in a busy spot.
See who takes you up on your offer.
Going out on a limb here, but we're guessing it will be uncomfortable...for lots of reasons.
But that's not necessarily a bad thing, right?
Not if you invite Jesus along.

## AND EVEN GRITTIER

Up the ante.

Turn your sign over and write, "Free hugs and affirmations."

You've now committed yourself to share, not only hugs but also kind words, with people you've never met.

You'll be handing out sincere compliments. Positive observations. Upbeat inspiration.

Perhaps even insights shared with you courtesy of the Holy Spirit.

Every encounter is an adventure, one in which you lean on Jesus.

And that's the very definition of growing grit.

## TALK WITH JESUS

Jot your thoughts about...

- **What did these experiences teach you about yourself?**

- **What did you discover about Jesus?**

- **In what ways was this experience hard...and good?**

- **Where was the spiritual grit in these experiences? Is it easier to offer affirming words or affirming actions? Explain.**

# LEAN INTO HARD CONVERSATIONS

Peter's worried about Jesus.

Lately, Jesus has talked about going to Jerusalem, dying, and rising from the dead. It's depressing, and furthermore, it's scaring away the crowds.

Whatever happened to water-into-wine Jesus? The Jesus who scooped up kids and gave James and John a hard time about their tempers? That's the Jesus Peter loves following.

But this new Jesus? The one spending more and more time alone in the hills, praying?

That guy's scaring Peter.

So Peter takes Jesus aside for a little man-to-man chat.

Peter assures Jesus there's no need for worry because none of Jesus' predictions will come true. No Jerusalem, no dying, no coming back from the tomb. If Jesus sticks with Peter, it'll all be fine.

That's when Jesus snaps back with something sharp and unfiltered.

"Get away from me, Satan! You are a dangerous trap to me. You are seeing things merely from a human point of view, not from God's" (Matthew 16:23).

If that sounds harsh, there's a reason: It is. Here's Peter, trying to help, and he gets his head handed to him. What has he done that's so wrong?

Peter doesn't see that Jesus has no choice but face the cross if he's to reconcile God and mankind. Jesus is going to Jerusalem because it's part of God's plan.

And along comes Peter suggesting Jesus abandon that plan, something Satan would love. At the moment, Peter and Satan are on the same page.

Peter's heart may be in the right place, but that doesn't change the fact that he's completely, dangerously misreading the situation.

So Jesus sets him straight.

It takes spiritual grit to journey with Jesus. And it takes a special measure of that grit to stay when Jesus has called you a devil to your face.

Peter is at a crossroads. He can get offended and leave, as many before him have, or choose to keep following Jesus.

He chooses Jesus...and turns his face toward Jerusalem.

Peter's a lot like you—and the rest of us who tag along after Jesus.

He's a work in progress.

More than once Peter requires a midcourse correction to keep him on track, and some of those come in the form of pointed conversations. Peter isn't alone; all the disciples are occasionally on the receiving end of tough-love conversations with Jesus.

But even as Jesus puts Peter in his place, Peter feels it: love. Jesus loves him enough to pause and deal with him. To correct, confront, encourage.

Jesus is building spiritual grit in Peter, and as hard as that can be at times, Peter loves Jesus for it.*

How about you? How do you respond when Jesus is a little (or a lot) hard on you? Do you see that as love...or something else?

*Read the entire account in Matthew 16:13-28.

You'll need two pieces of paper, a pen, and a match.

Ready?

Do this: On one sheet of paper, write five things about yourself that are true. Undeniably true—you know them to be fact because you've had them confirmed time and again.

Maybe it's that you've got a great sense of humor. Or that you're a gifted pianist. Or a solid friend.

Five things. Put them in writing.

On the other sheet of paper, write five things about yourself that aren't true—but you find yourself believing sometimes.

That at heart you're a failure. That you're a fraud. That if people really knew you they'd walk away from you.

Put those in writing, too.

Now invite Jesus to have a hard conversation with you about both lists.

Ask him how he wants to use those things on the first list to bring him honor and to enrich your life in the process.

Ask him to speak the truth to you about the second list.

Is there anything there that's partially true? Is there any part of what you've written that needs grit-fueled transformation from the inside out?

Now burn the second list. You don't need it; Jesus is on the case.

## AND EVEN GRITTIER

This will take a bit of planning. You'll need a full-length mirror and a great deal of privacy.

First, put the mirror in a place you won't—can't—be disturbed.

Second, strip down to your underwear.

Now look in the mirror and—out loud—describe what you see. When you're finished, keep reading. We can wait...

All done? Here's what you did: You described every flaw you saw. Every pimple, wart, and scar. Because that's what we do.

When we have frank conversations with ourselves, we're nearly always critical.

No wonder we so seldom have hard conversations with ourselves.

Now do this: Describe what *Jesus* sees when he looks at you. Who *Jesus* sees. How is his description different from yours?

## TALK WITH JESUS

Jot your thoughts about...

- **What did you discover about how you view yourself?**

- **What did you discover about how Jesus views you?**

- **In what ways was this experience hard...and good?**

- **Where was the spiritual grit in these experiences? Why is it important to know the truth about yourself?**

Jesus had no problem having a hard conversation with Peter.

That's what love does. When it senses a rift in a relationship, it addresses it. When there's an untruth, love drags it out into the light to examine it.

Not harshly...but firmly.

Not out of anger...but because love doesn't do well in the darkness. It needs honesty and transparency. It breathes best in light, not shadow.

Do this: Read aloud this passage from Psalm 139:24: "Point out anything in me that offends you, and lead me along the path of everlasting life."

Now read it again and mean it this time.

Listen and watch carefully for the next few days. What's Jesus pulling into the light for you to see?

What's the hard conversation he's wanting to have with you?

## AND EVEN GRITTIER

If you hear from Jesus, call another Jesus-follower and share what Jesus dragged into the light.

Be honest.

Be transparent.

And be willing to have your friend pray with and for you.

## TALK WITH JESUS

Jot your thoughts about...

- **What did these days of being open to a hard conversation with Jesus teach you about yourself?**

- What did you discover about Jesus?

- In what ways was this experience hard...and good?

- Where was the spiritual grit in these experiences? What freedoms do you experience when Jesus moves something from darkness into the light?

# GIVE UP ON GETTING EVEN

James and John are *ticked*.

Things are already tense; Jesus and his disciples are on their way to Jerusalem, unsure how they'll be received. And as the group travels through Samaria, Jesus sends messengers ahead to a village so they're ready to take care of himself and his crew.

But Jesus isn't welcome there, not if he's on his way to Jerusalem. Apparently the bitter feelings Samaritans have for Jews include Jesus and the disciples.

Yet again in Jesus' life, there's going to be no room in the inn.

James and John urge Jesus to go full Sodom and Gomorrah on the village, calling down fire from heaven to teach the inhospitable Samaritans a lesson they'll never forget, assuming they live through it at all.

Jesus not only doesn't do as they want, but Luke reports, "Jesus turned and rebuked them" (Luke 9:55). Some early manuscripts add, "For the Son of Man has not come to destroy people's lives, but to save them."

So much for James and John evening the score with the Samaritans for turning them away.*

James and John aren't the only ones keeping score and getting even—we do it, too. And let's admit it: It feels good. We applaud when bad guys get what they deserve.

But getting even isn't something Jesus has ever delegated to his disciples. Not to James and John, and not to us. Someone

*Read the entire account in Luke 9:51-56.*

else will make sure evildoers face the consequences of their actions. That's covered without our help.

And there's the tension where spiritual grit is built: choosing to give up on getting even.

Choosing to tear up the score card and walk away from demanding justice.

That's hard stuff—especially when you could get away with getting even or imposing a little punishment. Holding your fire when righteous indignation is pushing you to pull the trigger is remarkably difficult.

And it's the very thing Jesus does daily.

Because, while he loves those Samaritans in the village ahead, they *are* rejecting him. And while he loves the disciples sauntering along beside him, it's *their* sins that are taking him to the cross.

Jesus has given up on getting even so he can grab hold of something else: forgiveness.

The good news for the Samaritan villagers was this: James and John didn't have the power to call down fire from heaven. Had that been possible, the village would have been a smoking crater within minutes.

And here's the good news for you: While Jesus *does* have the power to direct fire and brimstone your way, he's offering you something else.

Something just as powerful but far more redemptive.

He's offering you forgiveness.

## GRIT GROWER 30: HOLD YOUR FIRE

There was a time when getting even required squaring off for a duel, or at least a fistfight.

But that's so last century.

Now we've got the internet.

You simply find someone's social media account and post a scathing review. You describe in detail what the person did and destroy a reputation. You can make accusations anonymously. You can take your best shot and then walk away.

But that's not what disciples do.

Disciples follow Jesus...and he didn't take revenge.

Do this: Find a social media account of someone who's hurt you. Look at the happy faces in the photos posted there. Read the list of accomplishments and notice how carefully the public persona has been cultivated.

Now imagine what you could write to set the picture right.

And don't do it. Instead, hold your fire.

Walk away.

## AND EVEN GRITTIER

Jesus said, "Bless those who curse you. Pray for those who hurt you" (Luke 6:28).

That's going one better than simply not taking revenge. It's being loving toward people you prefer to hate.

But you're a disciple who's following Jesus. You're on a path that led him to pray from the cross for the very people who were torturing him.

That's grit...and that's who you follow.

Why would you think he'd lead you anywhere but where he's gone himself?

That person whose indifference or anger has hurt you?

Pray for that person.

## TALK WITH JESUS

Jot your thoughts about...

- **What did you discover about yourself from these experiences?**

- How is what you just did like or unlike something Jesus has done?

- Where was the spiritual grit in these experiences? What do you have to overcome in yourself to "love your enemies"?

---

*"Dear friends, never take revenge. Leave that to the righteous anger of God. For the Scriptures say, 'I will take revenge; I will pay them back,' says the Lord" (Romans 12:19).*

---

## GRIT GROWER 31: STOP KEEPING SCORE

Take a wooden pencil and a piece of paper to a quiet spot where you can think and write without being disturbed.

On the paper list wrongs that have been done to you.

Not all of them—just those that have echoed through your life awhile. Abuse. Betrayal. Cheating. Lies that cost you dearly.

Be specific and detailed. Name names—you won't show this to anyone.

When you've finished (or run out of paper) read your list aloud. Let any feelings that come wash over and through you.

Invite Jesus to see your list through your eyes, eyes that may be filled with tears.

Ask him to help you see through his eyes, too. Sorrowful eyes that hold a spark of hope.

Then tear the paper into tiny pieces and snap the pencil in half.

You may not be ready to forgive yet—that's between you and Jesus. But you can decide to quit keeping score.

You can take a step toward trusting that God will make right what others made wrong.

## AND EVEN GRITTIER

Go someplace you can see a scoreboard. Your school's football or soccer field, a community gym, maybe even a bowling alley.

Once you're there, get comfortable and look long and hard at that scoreboard.

Ask Jesus this question: *When it comes to my getting even with others, what's the score?*

Expect to hear...nothing.

Because Jesus isn't big on your keeping score. He's way more interested in your discovering how to let him fuel your ability to forgive others.

So then ask him this question: *What needs to change in me so I won't worry about the score at all?*

You can expect he'll have a *lot* to say to you about that.

## TALK WITH JESUS

Jot your thoughts about...

- **What did you discover about yourself from these experiences?**

- **How did what you just did remind you of what Jesus has done?**

- **In what ways was this experience hard...and good?**

- Where was the spiritual grit in these experiences? Why is it so hard to stop keeping score?

## GRIT GROWER 32: A SCORE-SETTLING SCORE

Fire up your laptop or tablet and find some streaming music sites.

Your challenge: Find a song that captures how you feel about walking away from settling a score.

Maybe the thought of letting someone get away with something angers you. It seems so very unfair.

Or it disappoints you—you've been looking forward to payback.

Perhaps not getting revenge makes you happy, frightened, or something else.

Whatever you feel, find a song that reflects that feeling.

Play it—loudly.

If it has lyrics, sing along.

This is the soundtrack of your life at the moment...and a way to tell Jesus how you're feeling.

## AND EVEN GRITTIER

Field trip time again—this time to a cemetery.

Find the oldest section and walk among the headstones.

Notice the names. Do the math as you read the dates of births and deaths, consider lives lived and lives cut short.

So many people.

And none of them care any longer about who once angered them or who owed them a coin, compliment, or consideration.

That list of debts was erased on the last day carved on each tombstone. Getting even no longer mattered.

A thought: If death can erase the need to get even, how might something a bit less lethal do the same thing? How might forgiveness? How might love?

Ask Jesus what it's costing you to carry around your list of paybacks and what he'd have you do with it.

## TALK WITH JESUS

Jot your thoughts about...

- **What did you discover about yourself as you considered getting even?**

- **What did you discover about Jesus?**

- **In what ways was this experience hard...and good?**

- **Where was the spiritual grit in these experiences? What, if anything, has changed in you?**

# DON'T WORRY

When Jesus tells a crowd—one including his disciples—not to worry, they wonder if he's lost it. Because they're dealing with a few worry-worthy issues in their lives.

For starters, most of them are poor.

That whole "Give us this day our daily bread" request that Jesus tucks into his model prayer is real; many people shuffling around in Jesus' audience are literally unsure where their next meal will come from.

Which explains one reason there's such excitement whenever Jesus multiplies fish and bread and provides an all-you-can-eat buffet.

Plus, there's this: Their future is shaky at best.

Jews in Jesus' audience are never sure what might set off the Roman soldiers patrolling their neighborhoods. One wrong look, one cross word, any misunderstanding—the Romans have plenty of crosses they can pull out at a moment's notice.

Still, Jesus says this:

"You cannot serve God and be enslaved to money.

"That is why I tell you not to worry about everyday life—whether you have enough food and drink, or enough clothes to wear.

"Isn't life more than food, and your body more than clothing?

"Look at the birds. They don't plant or harvest or store food in barns, for your heavenly Father feeds them. And aren't you far more valuable to him than they are?

"Can all your worries add a single moment to your life?" (Matthew 6:24-27).*

Great advice, Jesus...but it's hard not to think about money when you're worried about feeding your family. If Jesus would multiply some silver coins instead of bread, a great deal of worry would evaporate instantly.

Besides, worrying is what some of us do best.

Fast forward and Jesus is sending his 12 disciples out into the world to do ministry. And he's allowing them to take with them... nothing.

No money. No food. No clothes other than what's on their backs.

All they get is a walking stick—period.

Once again, it seems Jesus is deliberately allowing a worrisome situation to continue. What's he up to?

Perhaps this: Spiritual grit grows when his disciples are forced to rely on Jesus rather than themselves. As positive as self-reliance can be, it's not the point of spiritual grit. In fact, it can seriously undermine it.

Spiritually gritty people rely on Jesus, not themselves. The strength and character they develop serves them well, but it never diverts their gaze from Jesus.

Jesus' first disciples discovered that truth, and it's waiting for the rest of us Jesus-followers to discover, too. You included.

The ability to set aside worry doesn't come from being so strong that nothing can harm you. You'll never be that strong. Rather, it comes from following Someone who's so strong that you can never be pried from the safety of his grasp, never be separated from him and the eternal life he offers you.

When you're with Jesus, you never have to worry.

Because you're with Jesus.

## GRIT GROWER 33: TELL A FRIEND

Tell a friend what you worry about most.

Is it money? health? relationships? What pegs your worry meter, and what do you think drives that worry?

*Read the entire account in Matthew 6:19-34.

Have the conversation, and then ask your friend to pray for you.

Right now, not later.

And out loud so you can hear what God's hearing. So you can soak up the encouragement that comes with knowing God is aware of what's worrying you.

## AND EVEN GRITTIER

Get thee to a waiting room.

At the Department of Motor Vehicles, a pharmacy, or a hospital. Anywhere you're not required to sign in and can sit without being booted out.

Then...wait.

Wait for five minutes...then ten...wait an hour if you want. Nothing will happen. You won't be called to the counter; your number will never appear on the monitor.

And that's exactly what you're doing when you worry: You're waiting for something that may not happen.

While you're waiting, invite Jesus to sit with you.

Maybe there's something he wants to say to you about worry.

## TALK WITH JESUS

Jot your thoughts about...

- **What did you discover about yourself as you considered worry? as your friend prayed for you?**


- **What did you discover about Jesus?**

- In what ways was this experience hard...and good?


- Where was the spiritual grit in these experiences? What's a practical way for you to hand Jesus your worries?


## GRIT GROWER 34: BUBBLE WRAP

Do this: Use bubble wrap to encase the most important item in your room.

It can be anything, or anyone, as long as it's precious to you. Step back to admire your work.

Invite Jesus to stand at your elbow and take a look, too.

A question: How much do you worry about harm coming to what's precious to you? Does that worry set off your emotional Richter scale, or doesn't it cross your mind?

And how much do you worry about your relationships—especially your friendship with Jesus? What do you do to protect that friendship?

There's no need to worry about Jesus drifting away from your friendship. He's all-in—always.

So abide. Just abide.

Remain connected to Jesus, and he'll give you the grit to abide in him.

## AND EVEN GRITTIER

Give something away—something you worry you might lose one day.

A framed photograph, that first-grade spelling bee ribbon you can't bear to throw out—anything that matters to you.

Whatever it is, however significant it is to you, hand it to a friend who's long admired it...or drop it into a Goodwill bin.

Hard to even imagine, isn't it?

But the truth is, no amount of worry makes your treasure yours forever. Or protects it from all that can harm it. There's no true security other than the security you'll find in Jesus, and he's way more interested in people than he is in your coin collection.

So...will you do it?

## TALK WITH JESUS

Jot your thoughts about...

- **What did you discover about yourself as you pondered worry and trust?**

- **What did you discover about Jesus?**

- **In what ways was this experience hard...and good?**

- **Where was the spiritual grit in these experiences? How do you experience freedom in the midst of worry?**

## GRIT GROWER 35: WORRIES, DISSECTED

Dissect one worry that's keeping you up at night. Break it down into smaller pieces.

That test you're scared of flunking? The one you fear might torpedo your GPA?

You need to pass it, so make a list:

• Talk with your teacher and ask for extra help.
• Study—with someone else around to keep you focused.
• Write and take a pretest to make sure you've mastered the material.

Worries grow strong in the absence of action. And they grow stronger still when you don't invite Jesus into the situations that worry you.

Because look at each of those steps above.

Which one is bigger or more powerful than Jesus?

None. So don't face your worries alone. Take Jesus along.

He has the grit to stick with you and the power to fix what's broken.


## AND EVEN GRITTIER

Light up a room.

*Really* light it—drag in lamps from all over the house. Open the drapes and throw wide the shutters. Even flip on that flashlight you keep in the junk drawer.

Then jot on a sheet of paper the worry you told your friend about (Grit Grower 33). Lay that paper on the floor, and aim as much light as possible directly at it.

Ask Jesus to look at the worry you wrote down.

That should be easy because you've lit it well enough to be visible from space and he's considerably closer than that.

Then ask Jesus to flood your heart with peace, just as you've flooded the room with light.

To remove worry from your heart and mind even if the situation prompting that worry isn't resolved.

To replace worry with trust.
And amen.

## TALK WITH JESUS

Jot your thoughts about...

- **What did you discover about yourself through these experiences?**

- **What did you discover about Jesus?**

- **In what ways were these experiences hard...and good?**

- **Where was the spiritual grit in these experiences? How do you grow when you give your worries to Jesus?**

# LET PEOPLE KNOW YOU'RE WITH JESUS

In the end, Jesus' first disciples run away rather than admit they know him.

Hearts pounding, shame coursing through them, they hide their faces. Keep to the shadows. Anything to avoid following Jesus to the cross.

Even Peter—loyal-to-a-fault Peter—swears by all that's holy he doesn't know Jesus, has never met the man being brutally beaten in the high priest's house.

Peter bolts, leaving both his self-respect and Jesus behind.

And as Peter abandons Jesus, his master's words ring in his ears. Just hours before, Jesus leaned forward at their shared Passover meal, and said this:

"And you must also testify about me because you have been with me from the beginning of my ministry" (John 15:27).

Testify?

The dozen disciples can't even be *located*. They're hiding in the darkest corners of Jerusalem they can find.

But what choice do they have? In the days following Jesus' crucifixion, being associated with him is risking being labeled a heretic, perhaps an enemy of the state. Either accusation can prove fatal.*

In some parts of the world, the same risk remains today: Taking a public stand for Jesus can cost you your life.

*Read the entire account in Matthew 26:47-75.*

And yet Jesus insists that those who follow him do so openly, not as secret admirers but in full view. Jesus was prepping his closest disciples for a short-term mission trip when he said this to them:

"Everyone who acknowledges me publicly here on earth, I will also acknowledge before my Father in heaven. But everyone who denies me here on earth, I will also deny before my Father in heaven" (Matthew 10:32-33).

In other words, no traveling incognito. Jesus' disciples were to clearly associate themselves with him.

If you happen to be a missionary serving in a society where open identification with Jesus will get you beheaded, let's assume you get a pass on this. You *are* openly identifying with Jesus; just doing so one trusted person at a time.

But for the rest of us, Jesus' demand might be awkward.

Yes, we follow him...but we aren't sure we want everyone to know. Christians as a tribe have a difficult reputation: We're often viewed as narrow-minded, intolerant, hypocritical, and homophobic. Do you really want to plaster that sort of label on your chest? It may be wrong, it may be a stereotype, but it's believed nonetheless.

Odd, isn't it? Everyone talks about the spiritual grit required to have a personal relationship with Jesus but it's living out a *public* relationship with him that can get you killed. Or at least make you uncomfortable.

Yet Jesus insists we acknowledge him—and with more than T-shirts. He's looking for us to stand up for him not only with words but also with actions.

That's what he's done—and is doing—for us.

How can we do less for him?

It's a question that's been asked of Jesus' followers for generations: If you were put on trial for following Jesus, would there be enough evidence to convict you?

That question is usually trotted out as a hammer, meant to smack an audience into doing more, saying more, giving more. But intent aside, it's actually a fair question.

Jesus asks that you acknowledge him—that you remove any doubt about your allegiance to him. That you state clearly who he is in your life.

If that's happening, it's going to leave some evidence in its wake.

Not just words, but lives that have been touched.

Not just good intentions, but actions that have been taken.

So picture asking Jesus that question: *If I were put on trial for following you, would there be enough evidence to convict me?*

And what might he say if he were called to the stand to testify on your behalf?

## GRIT GROWER 36: TAKE A STAND

If it's election season, put a sign in your yard or window declaring your preference for a certain candidate or issue.

And election season or not, fire up social media and link to a church site or another Christian site.

Take a stand.

Go public.

In whatever way Jesus leads you, get off the bench and into the game.

See what happens.

## AND EVEN GRITTIER

Go stand alongside Jesus.

Do it at an institution in your community you think has turned its back on Jesus.

Maybe it's a bar. A government office. Anywhere you, judging as lovingly as you can, believe has given up on Jesus.

Stand in the shadow of that place and quietly ask Jesus to be with the people who are in its circle of influence.

Be legal—stay on the sidewalk or other space open to the public. And don't take along bullhorns, bombast, or signs. They won't be welcome, and you don't need them.

Simply pray. Quietly stand with Jesus.

By the way, you can be sure he's there because no matter how thoroughly people walk away from him, he doesn't walk away from them.

And if you were wrong and the organization also honors Jesus but you just don't know it?

He's still there.

Either way, you're standing with him.

## TALK WITH JESUS

Jot your thoughts about…

- **What did you discover about yourself as you considered taking a public stand for Jesus?**

- **What did you discover about Jesus as you asked him about taking a stand?**

- **In what ways was this experience hard…and good?**

- **Where was the spiritual grit in these experiences? How did you grow from them?**

## GRIT GROWER 37: SAY IT WITH CHALK

Buy sidewalk chalk, and in front of where you live, draw the following on the sidewalk or street:

"Someone who loves Jesus lives here."

You won't get in trouble for vandalism: One rainstorm or hosing will wash away the chalk. And in many places in the world, you won't get in trouble for sharing what you believe: Free speech is a wonderful thing.

Still...how does it feel being that bold about your faith? to be so clear about who you are and whose you are?

## AND EVEN GRITTIER

Someone famously said, "Preach the gospel at all times and when necessary use words."

That's your grit-growing challenge: Treat others in such a way today that they're prompted to ask what's different about you, what's fueling your kindness, compassion, and empathy.

When they ask, tell them: You're following Jesus.

## TALK WITH JESUS

Jot your thoughts about...

- **What did you discover about yourself as you declared your connection to Jesus?**


- **What did you discover about Jesus?**


- **In what ways was this experience hard...and good?**


- **Where was the spiritual grit in these experiences? What's your next step in standing for Jesus?**

# BE UNIFIED

When Jesus prays that his followers find unity, the disciples aren't surprised. Jesus has pushed them to get along for years, ever since he called them to follow him.

Because really, the only thing the disciples have in common is Jesus.

Some of them knew each other before Jesus recruited them. James and John are brothers, as are Peter and Andrew. But anyone who's been raised with a brother will tell you that doesn't always mean you're unified.

Sometimes brothers are the *least* united people you're likely to find.

And the other disciples Jesus throws together? He couldn't pick less likely people to call to unity.

Take Matthew and Simon the Zealot.

Matthew's a tax collector. Was one, anyway, before quitting to follow Jesus.

He worked for the Romans and, with a soldier or two at his side, made sure his neighbors handed over their fair share of taxes to Rome. Their fair share and a bit more to line his own pockets.

And Simon? He's a zealot, a member of one of the nationalist groups dedicated to evicting, killing, or maiming as many Romans—and Jews who've sold out to Rome—as possible.

Jesus recruits both men...and then has them travel together. Two men who previously wouldn't consider being in the same room are expected to work alongside each other and to be more than colleagues. They're to become brothers in the best, kingdom sense of the word.

It's not listed as a miracle, but Matthew and Simon heading off side by side and then both coming back alive? That's right up there with water into wine.

Jesus values unity so highly that, as he prays for his disciples just hours before he's arrested, he prays this:

"I pray that they will all be one, just as you and I are one—as you are in me, Father, and I am in you. And may they be in us so that the world will believe you sent me...May they experience such perfect unity that the world will know that you sent me and that you love them as much as you love me" (John 17:21, 23).

Clearly, unity is important to Jesus. But why?

Because it signals to the world that Jesus is legit. The change that happens in his disciples proves there's power in their passion for Jesus.

Besides, Jesus has ever and always been about relationships. He's calling his disciples not only to himself, but to one another. His kingdom isn't about only a new order but also a new way for God and people to connect, and for people to connect with one another.*

And then there's this: Relationships are a great place for grit to grow.

They require listening, compassion, forgiveness. Grit-growers, all.

Relationships are challenging, calling out the best in you and revealing your worst.

And they pave the way, ultimately, to a unity that reflects the relationship Jesus has with the Father and the Holy Spirit. *That's* what real unity looks like when it's all grown up.

Is getting there hard? Ask Matthew and Simon—they'll tell you.

Unity requires a passion for Jesus that's so strong it accepts who he accepts and serves those he serves. It takes letting Jesus teach you to soften your heart and hold your tongue.

And is it worth the effort?

Ask Jesus.

*Read the entire account in John 17:1-26.

## GRIT GROWER 38: NEIGHBORHOOD DIRECTORY

One way to build unity is to connect people who live near one another. People who live in your apartment block, say, or whose houses line your street.

Go knock on doors and explain that you're assembling a neighborhood directory, one that will help neighbors get to know one another better.

Give each neighbor a copy of your directory information, already filled out: name, address, phone number, email, hobbies, any odd jobs you do for fun or money, and a few lines explaining where you're from and how long you've lived where you live.

Ask each neighbor to fill out a similar sheet for the directory, and promise to give a directory to each one after you've completed it.

Congratulations: You've met your neighbors. And helped build unity.

Plus, you now know who might need a babysitter or car washer.

## AND EVEN GRITTIER

Invite your neighbors to a hot dog roast—at your place.

Get your hands on a portable fire pit and park it out front where everyone can see it. Then go buy enough drinks, hot dogs, buns, and condiments to feed the masses. And snag some wire hangers, too—you'll need plenty for heating hot dogs.

Did we mention this is going to cost a few bucks?

Invite your neighbors in advance and ask for an RSVP.

Point out this is a tasty way to connect with people who live nearby but might as well live on another planet insofar as conversations are concerned.

Make it fun: music, laughter, games for the kids.

And hot dogs. Lots and lots of hot dogs.

# TALK WITH JESUS

Jot your thoughts about...

- **What did you discover about yourself—and your neighbors?**

- **How might Jesus suggest you invest in these new relationships? What did he say when you asked him?**

- **In what ways was this experience hard...and good?**

- **Where was the spiritual grit in these experiences? For you, what's the hardest thing about initiating relationships?**

**GRIT GROWER 39:** UNCOMMON COMMONALITIES, COMMON UNCOMMONALITIES

You'll need another Jesus-follower for this, so call someone you know only marginally. A friend of a friend. That person who's new to your church or youth group. Just make sure it's not an old friend you already know well.

All set?

Perfect! Do this: Take three minutes to identify as many things as possible that the two of you have in common. Not the obvious stuff (you both have noses) but things that are a bit deeper (you both love the smell of coffee).

Three minutes. See how much you have in common.

Now take three minutes to identify your differences: food preferences, sports teams, musicians.

Then discuss this: In what ways does your shared belief in Jesus unite the two of you? Does that shared belief trump the differences you identified?

Why—or why not?

## AND EVEN GRITTIER

This is going to be fun. It may ding your dignity a bit, but it'll be worth it.

Buy a bottle of bubbles—the kind that come with a wand.

Recruit a friend to sit with you on a park bench and take turns blowing bubbles. Lots of bubbles. Offer passersby opportunities to give it a try, too, especially people who look like they could use some cheering up.

And small kids. Small kids *love* bubbles.

Run that bottle right down until you've got nothing but fumes in it. Then talk about this: How has this experience affected your friendship? Do you feel closer to this friend...or more distant?

We're betting the experience further cements your friendship, that you'll enjoy this memory together for years.

What's true with your bubble buddy is also true with Jesus: When you have an adventure with him—even a silly one—you grow closer to him.

And your friendship with Jesus is ultimately your best—and only—source of spiritual grit.

What adventures have you shared with Jesus lately?

Up for one?

# TALK WITH JESUS

Jot your thoughts about...

- **What did you discover about yourself through these experiences?**

- **What did you discover about Jesus?**

- **In what ways was this experience hard...and good?**

- **Where was the spiritual grit in these experiences? What is it about an adventure that strengthens you?**

## GRIT GROWER 40: LOSE THE PHONE, PAL

Put your phone away.

Don't use it to distract yourself as you stand in line, take the bus, or fill spare moments. Instead, look up and smile.

Make contact with the people around you.

Risk striking up a conversation.

See what you have in common with the rest of humanity. And as you interact, keep an ear cocked for Jesus' whisper letting you know how you might serve or bless someone.

That listening you're doing?

It's focusing on Jesus. Abiding in him. Building grit.

## AND EVEN GRITTIER

What most people think of as listening is just waiting for the chance to talk.

Listening—*really* listening—is an act of unity. Always. Every time.

So today sit down with someone and do the hard work of listening. Of hearing what she's saying and noticing how she's feeling. Of asking follow-up questions to give her the space to explore her story more deeply.

You're giving her a rare and priceless gift: your complete attention.

She's giving you an equally valuable thing: She's sharing her life.

Ask Jesus who he wants you to listen to today.

Then see what it takes to make it happen.

## TALK WITH JESUS

Jot your thoughts about...

- **What did you discover about yourself as a listener?**

- **What did you discover about Jesus as a listener?**

- **In what ways was this experience hard...and good?**

- **Where was the spiritual grit in these experiences? How have you grown as a result?**

Ask Jesus.

He'll tell you.

You're following, right? That's what disciples do, so there's not much for you to plan.

Just keep your eyes on Jesus and do your best to keep up.

Bless you on your journey.

# NOTES

# NOTES

GROWING SPIRITUAL GRIT
FOR TEENAGERS

# NOTES

# NOTES

GROWING SPIRITUAL GRIT
FOR TEENAGERS

# NOTES

# NOTES

GROWING SPIRITUAL GRIT
FOR TEENAGERS

# NOTES

# TAKE THE NEXT STEP TO GROW YOUR SPIRITUAL GRIT

ADVANCE YOUR JOURNEY INTO GREATER ENDURANCE, CHARACTER, CONFIDENCE, AND HOPE WITH RICK LAWRENCE'S BOOK *SPIRITUAL GRIT.*

## *SPIRITUAL GRIT* INCLUDES:

- Ways to access the strength needed to live a resilient life through a greater dependence on Jesus.

- Biblical stories of those who grew a "grit backbone" through their interactions with Jesus.

- An extensive menu of life habits that fertilize grit, plus a method for identifying habits that undermine it.

- A way to assess your own spiritual grit.

Without Jesus, grit is little more than a gimmick. With Jesus, grit can infuse the world—and our lives—with hope.

**Available now at Christian retailers and SpiritualGritBook.com.**